Do You Hear What I Sing

Poetry Books by Livingston Rossmoor

A Stream Keeps Running (2013)

Do You Hear What I Sing (2014)

A Journey in the Animal Kingdom (2014)

A Never-Ending Battle (2015)

When Ruby was Still in My Arms (2015)

I Hear the Ocean Landing (2016)

The Thunder Was So Mad (2017)

I Found Ruth Tonight (2017)

Collected Triplets (2018)

Selected Ballads, Villanelles, Couplets,
Tanka Sequences, Cinquains & Triplets (2018)

Selected Sonnets (2018)

Selected Poems 2002-2017 (2018)

Also by Livingston Rossmoor

Old Buddy Chang (2001)
(13 short stories)

One Ray of Light at Dawn (2002)
(poetry & prose)

DVD & CD-One Ray of Light at Dawn (2003)
(12 Lyrics & Melodies)

One Ray of Light at Dawn (2005)
(Book of Music Scores)

The Beauty and the Ugly (2006)
(poetry & prose)

DVD-Perpetual Stream (2007)
(10 Lyrics & Melodies)

Perpetual Stream (2009)
(Book of Music Scores)

Do You Hear What I Sing

Poems by   Livingston Rossmoor

Published by
EGW Publishing
(since 1979)

I dedicate this book to my grandchildren:
Scarlet Shinkle, Max Shinkle, Miles Shinkle,
Sullivan Lin, Bowie Lin, Lincoln Sandler,
Leo Sandler, Ruby Sandler

and to my dear wife, Grace.

I particularly wish to thank
Lisa Rigge, Charles Sandler and
Chris Slaughter for their suggestions and
encouragement.

EGW Publishing (since 1979)

ISBN 978-0-916393-33-5

www.egwpublishing.com

Once upon a time,
dinosaurs ruled the world,
huge bodies, loud noises,
as though no one else mattered.

And now, humans rule the world,
abundant small bodies,
even louder cacophony,
as though birds are in the lost kingdom.

I think, birds choose
to speak softly to balance
human clamor,
at this time, on this planet.

In this book, I choose to amplify their voices, pride, meditations, thoughts, avowals and feelings to silence human noises.

Table of Contents

Title   Page

There is symbolic as well as actual beauty...

Hope is the thing with feathers that
perches in the soul
and sings the tunes without the words
and never stops at all.

Emily Dickinson

Jonathan Livingston Seagull

Scavenging crabs and worms on the beach,
they follow the same routine to squabble for
small fish, bicker and brawl. That'll never reach
the profundity of how to espouse and soar.

Every seagull has their own destiny,
each journey is unique and rare,
flying to a higher plane in harmony
is the felicity beyond joy and flair.

Sky is not the limit, and there is no
heaven until the arrival of the drum beats.
I ascend above and beyond every foe
with daring and triumphant aerial feats.

Fly, fly, the calling, into the clouds,
resound in the doldrums of the crowds.

Release Dove

It's hard to say if I'm a pigeon or a dove.
I'm bred to look good, to open a ceremony,
to salute an important milestone in life,
to start a loving matrimony.

I am a messenger of spirit.
I symbolize the hope of a new beginning,
serenity of the deepest kind,
love and harmony of family values.
Avowal of everlasting truth.

I sooth and quiet
troubled and worried thoughts,
enable them to find the renewal
and the silence of soul in this flurried world.
A stillness, not to hurry as usual.

Not too high or too fast,
I keep my peace during my flight,
let the wind take me to a new height.

Hummingbird

I dream at night and reverie is my life,
pretending to work hard, I flap each wing
and heed every rumor, the gossip is rife.
Grass is greener over the fence as they sing.

To fulfill my impulses, I dash to
anywhere at the speed equal to my fickle
resolution, forward, backward, every clue,
every passing caprice, I'm on call to stickle.

I am humming so fast, making myself dizzy.
Starving all the time, I'm hungry for nectar.
Perching, resting, then buzzing and busy.
With earful of cues, I'm a bustling detector.

A dream to turn my instinct to vision.
If I can avoid the next collision.

Swan

I am a rare bird. I am a symbol,
an image, an icon of fidelity and love.
Princess transforms into swan, so does nimble
prince. I'm quiet, pure, peaceful like a white dove.

Ask Tchaikovsky or Yeats, there are more
ballets, music, poems written about me than
others in the kingdom. With elegant lore,
through generations, everyone is a swan fan.

To mate for life is our nature, divorce is not
in our future. Humans study but never
learn from us. My life is simple, tie the knot,
no matter what, we are in unison forever.

A strong will, hard to find in the throng.
Stay true to my fame, till I sing my swan song.

Homing Pigeon

(When Cher Ami died, she was mounted, and is a permanent
exhibit at the national museum of American history in the
Smithsonian Institute.)

I am bred for racing.
They called me thoroughbred of the sky.
I can carry messages over long distances
and be home on time, punctual, never tarry.

We contributed in World War One and Two.
Cher Ami, our kin, saved the lost battalion
of the 77th infantry division in 1918, a true hero.
She was mounted and exhibited with her medallion.

In Buckingham Palace, a grand ceremony
was held, saluting us for delivering vital plans
to the Allies in Normandy, a testimony
of bravery through the battlefields of our clans.

Now I can't fly faster than Internet or cell phone.
Still, my heart to my home is a pride of my own.

A poet is a nightingale, who sits in darkness and sings to cheer its own solitude with sweet sounds.

Percy Shelley

Nightingale

(Homer evokes the nightingale in The Odyssey. Wordsworth saw
the nightingale as an instance of natural poetic creation.
Nightingale became a voice of nature.
"Ode to a Nightingale" is a poem by John Keats.
"A Defense of Poetry" is written by Percy Shelley.)

I am born a poet, mesmerized by my voice,
invigorate the depressed souls and heal
their wounded hearts. And it is my choice
to lament melancholy if I so feel.

I breathe, dream and sleep on my poetry. I sing
day and night, live in dense foliage, out of sight.
Whistles, trills and gurgles on my wing.
Cling to my melodies and lyrics, a daily rite.

I sing the loudest in the sweet morning air.
Plain looking, I am no different than
those on the fences, until they hear the flair
of my crescendo, peaking through such a span.

Homer, Wordsworth, Keats and Shelley are my
dear friends, who share my joy, sorrow and sigh.

Skylark

There are more poets writing about me
than any other critter.
And a lyrical "lark ascending" for
orchestra and violin.
Heaven, earth, music and poems
as I dart and soar.

I earn it purely from my singing in flight.
Rising in the early morning,
brightening the sky.
"I represent joy, hope" they write,
and "freedom, inspiration" as I fly.

They see so much of themselves in me.
I am just an ordinary bird,
earth tone with mundane plumage.
They say "we are humble yet ascendant."
They all wish they can be just like me.

In climbing and descending,
you are what you sing.
Rise and fall, without a plot.
Just abide the fate,
accept the lot.

Common Loon

I am a musician. My native haunting call
sets the stage at dusk, right before sunset.
Silhouettes of trees, bits of daylight left,
the lake is so clear, so calm and no threat.

My yodeling sound actualizes the longing
of the soul, in touch with abandoned dreams,
forsaken desires, a sense of belonging,
an echo of unyielding and wearied screams.

A song of untamed exploration.
nostalgic in nature,
so far away, so nearby.
The call to reminisce the lingering aspiration.

"Where are you?" someone wails. "I am here."
is my reply. You'll hear and feel. Loud and clear.

Songbird

To sing or not to sing, that's not a choice.
I happen to be born with a song box.
In health, in sickness, joy or sorrow.

Does turmoil have a scale, one to ten?
It's a bygone truth, this world is unfair.
Crows screech, loons croon, owls hoot.

Turtles cannot sing, nor do they fly.
The line-up is impressive. Tanager, finch,
sparrow, wren, robin, canary or thrush?

No one knows the secret of inspiration.
Cuckoos reiterate toots, tinker birds repeat
hammering. Blackbirds bring the whole choir.

Judged by a few, are Oscars a fair game?
Nightingale, skylark, poet's love. Writers prefer
mockingbird. Who is the fairest of them all?

Super Lyrebird

Hermes invented the lyre to please Apollo.
Music has been discovered since then.
My fossil dates back to 15 million years ago.

Born with lyre as my tail is not a coincidence.
Who else can make so many
sounds and melodies?
Mimicking other birds' singing is nothing new.
I render with great fidelity,
and I create my own repertoires.
A superlative finesse with
variety and quality that is aureate.

I can mimic the alarm and engine of a car.
Camera shutter, chainsaw, crying baby,
rifle-shot, barking dog, I'm an imitating star.
It's unmatchable, there is no one like me.

The display of my tail fanned plumage
may come close to matching my song box.
It pomps with sixteen highly modified feathers,
splayed out like a lyre.

Memory, hearing, ears and brain,
I've got it all.
Copy, compose, I can echo every call.

Do you hear what I sing?

Cockatiel

Pretension is not an easy profession.
The intention is surmised and reckoned.
Orange cheeks, pumpkin color, I'm a real charm.

It is a cinch to smile when you are happy.
Mountain is set for the sea of clouds to invade.
Up or down, joy or strife, I whistle my greeting.

Fighting for freedom is a modern disease.
Balloons crave to fly to the moon and pop.
A tale of two cages, I prefer the small one.

The outside world is a beauty contest.
It is comical to read the regulations.
Affable with affection, I am such a chic.

Sword hides its glitz and smile in the sheath.
Of course, everyone finds his own home.
My crest tells it all. I don't harbor any emotions.

Canary

Any acapella competition, vibrato,
duet, trio in parody or rhapsody.
I breathe so fast that my staccato
is as smooth as a harmonious melody.

Gasp and respire as rapidly as I could,
carbon monoxide first kills and silences me.
Miners run for their lives if music should
stop. If you hear me no more, it's time to flee.

I live and sing to please everyone,
and die to guard the toiling miner.
A sentinel until the work is done.
I sacrifice myself, I am a diviner.

I belong to the heavens, and I'm born to sing,
to warble, rain or shine, winter or spring.

The butterfly counts not months but moments,
and has time enough.

Rabindranath Tagore

Butterfly

As though the allegory needs evidence
to enhance its poignancy, it may be short,
may be long, transforming in confidence,
a moment in life contrives to hold the fort.

Chorion's my armor, cuticle over cuticle,
hatch into larva after diapause and rest.
Hungry, quest for food, hours so critical.
I long to reach the crest and show my best.

I'm impelled to transform to pupa, to
metamorphose to butterfly. In a hurry
to blazon my alluring dress, I strew
every spore and pollen in a flurry.

The glaring shine is the highlight of my prime,
to testify a moment of truth lasting a lifetime.

Moth

(According to one report, a male moth can detect an odor
molecule of a female hormone seven miles away.)

I have nothing to dress up,
but I am sensitive to female sex hormones
a couple miles away.
We have 250,000 species.
We outnumber
the enchanting butterfly
by ten to one.

My hairy body makes me a great pollinator.
White flowers are my call,
I make them as fragrant as they can be.

Butterfly shows off under the sun,
I work the night shift for a week.
That is all the time I have to live.

Like all the good things,
fleeting and brief.
Life is too short for me.

Dragonfly

(In Europe, I am a devil. In Japan, I have my own dragonfly island.
I am a symbol of courage, strength and happiness. Big-time
poets, Basho, Bakusui and more wrote haiku about me. As many
haiku have been written as there are we dragonflies.)

At the end,

I am so glad,
I can show you my very best.
For 4 years, I live as a wingless nymph,
shedding skin, changing my look,
15 times.
Finally, I fly with my ultimate
make-up and dress
for a few days, weeks or months
before I die.

Brilliantly iridescent,
metallic colors,
conspicuous in flight.
It has been 300 million years
and counting.
I've never tired of
sacrificing,
incubating,
for the final moment.

All the best

at the end.

*Heard melodies are sweet, but those unheard
are sweeter.*

John Keats

Bald Eagle

I am a revered bird. Prominent on seals,
coinage, logos of federal agencies, stamp,
flag of the President and all wheels and deals.
I represent the United States. I'm the champ.

All the others change hands in four or eight years,
I am resolute on every picture, and in all
ceremonies. For better or worse, in fears
or calm, I am unique and remain tall.

Together, my mate and I build a nest
of sticks in the tree-tops, weighs up to a ton,
a massive home. Once paired, we settle and vest
until death. My loyalty, second to none.

I must confess, like humans, I am not
perfect, lurk and steal, sometimes, that's all I've got.

Bee

The sound of my buzzing is a symbol
of diligence, never getting tired, it is
steadfast and persistent, humming and nimble
with exertion, helping the world turn and whiz.

Petals and sepals extend their red
carpet welcome, pollens conjured to be
pollinated, marriages need matchmakers to spread
and drone the news, a glutton for work, that's me.

All these flowers depend on me to find
a match, they expound on the requirement,
grind the pedantic details into my mind,
endless requests delay my retirement.

Rumors and gossip, so much on my wings.
The mission summons all my queens and kings.

Hoopoe

I am a sacred bird in Ancient Egypt.
No one knows what's behind the veil.
Ancient Greeks named me king of birds.

A celebration to return to bare earth.
Sun hypnotizes in its own warmth.
I was depicted on the tombs of emperors.

Thousands of years of glorious history.
Giant barrel sponge witnesses it all.
It is just a part of bristlecone's life.

Upright crest, black and white stripes.
It's absurd to judge based on a look.
Crows screech, the only voice they were given.

There's no umbrage in the dialogue.
Is an honest criticism so hard to swallow?
I'm voted to become national bird of Isarel.

Ladybug

(5,000 species. The name Coccinellidae is derived from the Latin word coccineus meaning "scarlet." It is known as ladybird in Britain, and ladybug in America. "Ladybird" originated in Britain, where the insects became known as "Our Lady's bird." Mary, Our Lady, was often depicted wearing a red cloak in early paintings, and the spots of the seven-spot ladybird were said to symbolize her seven joys and seven sorrows.)

I like to wear bright red with black spotted coat.
My name ladybird links to Our Lady, a bond.
It must be a dream, I'm just a minuscule mote.
I became such a hit, touched by a magic wand?

I am so tiny with an oval-shaped dome,
deserving no attention. But farmers cheer
and love me. I eat plant-eating pests as I roam,
and consume five thousand aphids a year.

A symbol of good luck, heralding a time of
blessings, wishes, longings, and a higher goal
are now thinkable. Worries dissipate, love
is my motif, joy in the soul is the whole.

Call me any name you like, I'm not a starlet,
too old for that; ladybird, ladybug or Scarlet.

In the process of simplifying oneself, one often discovers the thing called voices.

Billy Collins

Cardinal

Colonists like my crest,
name me Cardinal.
I stay in the same place my entire life,
within a mile or two from my birth nest.
I feed and care for mother and babies,
I'm a good father, chasing out intruders.
Always standing by.
That is what I do best.

And listen, my mate is a true songster,
sing, sing with zest.

Most birds hate the city-growth.
We love the feeders in the park.
I thrive as the town grows,
build my parish,
expand my congregation.
Seven states selected me as their state bird.

I was given a name.
I work hard to live up to my fame.

Blue Jay

Perky crest, blue, white and black plumage,
good looking, nice voices, smart and sharp.
I am all over North America, colorful, loud,
even louder during the baseball season.
I root for the Toronto Blue Jays, of course,
and I'm very proud to cheer with the crowd.

I love acorns from oak trees.
I help to spread their growth
after the ice age.
Always near oaks in woodlot
and forest edge,
I also cruise through
towns, cities and parks.
Please do not lock me up in a cage.

I do migrate, no one, not even I,
knows when or why,
I may or may not bid good-bye.

Secretary Bird

It is a comfort to run in my own circle.
The contrast manifests in the selection.
Africa's my home. I run, fly, eat pests and snakes.

Guardian angel has wide span of wings.
Memory fades, remembrance remains.
35 countries put me on 65 stamps.

Distance-keeping is a profound craft.
Runners like to pursue from behind.
Fawn follows doe, stag hides in the woods.

It is quite an artistic achievement.
A pride to not get caught in the same trap.
Outside of Africa, no one knows me.

Name recognition is a farcical battle.
Motifs, flags, insignia, an ego trip.
My only wish is, change my name, please.

Baltimore Oriole

My bold orange and black plumage
sports the same colors as the old heraldic crest
of England's Baltimore family.
They gave the name to the city of Baltimore.

You are what you wear.
I became the state bird of Maryland,
their inspiration and the witty name
for the baseball team they all love.

I'm not born with a silver spoon in my mouth.
But I know how to dress up, when to appear.
To open the baseball season, I fly from the south.
I stay till the games are over and leave with a tear.

Sunshine I bring, and the spring.
As the wind rocks the cradle,
in my hanging nest, I sing.

Woodpecker

Before the sunrise, serene and still,
with no drill, the stage is set to nag,
to pick things apart, no song or trill,
no content, nor meaning, such a drag.

When I am working in the day time,
humans believe as though I've been
a naysayer all my life. My work is a chime.
I love to wake everyone up to join the din.

Never dawdle, I'm igneous to prove my point,
a tedious premonition, a perpetual knock
to please my soul. Poke and peek to joint
the rap and strike, a warning around the clock.

When the night is tranquil and at peace,
it's time to remind and repeat, never cease.

The truth of the matter is, the birds could very well live without us, but many - perhaps all - of us would find life incomplete, indeed almost intolerable without the birds.

Roger Tory Peterson

Scarlet Macaw

(Scarlet Macaw is the national bird of Honduras.)

I am the most beautiful parrot.
Bright red feathers and blue, yellow wings.
In my rainforest country,
I spread really wide.
Sing, sing,
with my comrades and chums,
fly, fly to the new height.

Hollow bones to buoy
and aid my flight,
I zoom through the evergreen jungle
with all my might.

One day, I was caught.
I sighed and cried.
Sky is still blue,
I can't see it any more.
The illegal parrot trade,
a handsome reward to catch me.
I was kidnapped in the bright daylight.

In the cage,
I crack seeds and nuts to kill time,
bored and miserable, I make noises,
the only voices
against the crime.
Sassy to show my personality,
and dislike of my sorry plight.

I begin to worry about my buddies.
They will be caught,
into different cages. Oh!
How I miss the rain,
the forest, the evergreen.
At night,
I dream and wish
someone would fight
to protect my right.

Hoatzin

Hoatzin means pheasant. Bizarre shape,
striking colors, unwary, no hurry.
I am Guyana's national bird.

I grow two claws on each of
my wings to avoid falling into water.
A miniature dinosaur's look-alike?

A unique digestive system generates
a manure-like odor. No one likes it.
A flat bad taste. A pungency of an old era?

All predators and humans dislike me.
A stinky bird. I survive longer than
any perfumes and imitators.

Wars, fires, heaven and hell.
Men come and go. Stench, fetor,
are my weapons. I live my easeful life.

Cuckoo

I have an absolute pitch, I sing
in the key of C in almost every call.
I whistle to herald the coming of spring,
and leave for Africa at the end of fall.

A repertoire of calls,
most people know.
A star, I am not.
I live in secrecy,
do not like to wow
or charm as on the stage
or on the spot.

Flying down to the host's nest,
I kick one out,
lay my egg and flit,
quiet, no shout.
I am a brood parasite.
Life is but a skit.

Cuck-oo,
hide and see,
can you hear?
Somewhere in the trees.
Mask and cover, cloak and harbor.
Life is lonely,
ditch, duck, deeper and deeper.
When I lose myself,
I pitch and call.
Cuck-oo,
Cuck-oo,
I still hear.

Bat

I'm the only mammal able to fly.
A kite in the wind, a drone in the sky.
Every man wishes he can fly.

A true sustained flight, not a glide.
Mountains, cliffs, caves and trees.
I am in every habitat, dark or bright.

More diseases are carried by mosquitos.
Men are sent to moon anytime they like.
I am the mosquito-killer sent by God.

Squirrels fly a little, possums glide.
Tiger chases a big bird into the sky.
I use echolocation to find my prey.

Ladybug bonds to Our Lady.
I became a hero since humans
invented a batman to fly like me.

There is no grief like the grief that does not speak.

Henry Wadsworth Longfellow

Giant Ibis

A huge majestic fowl, three feet tall,
native to marshes, veldts and forests,
I am Cambodia's national bird.

Bidding good-bye soon, I'm the first one
to leave the party, most endangered bird.
Sun will rise, but there is no home for me.

Drainage of wetlands for cultivation,
epidemic cutting of forest for rubber and
wood pulp. Human warfare and droughts.

What can I say? I am too strong, too big.
No place to hide. An easy target.
Hummingbirds need only bird feeders.

What else is new? A count-down has begun.
Swallow, finch, wren are everywhere.
Give me a smaller life, if there's a next life.

Vampire Bat

(3 out of 1,240 species of bat are vampire bats)

I weigh only two ounces. Still,
it sounds scary, I am the only mammal
that feeds entirely on blood.

I use teeth to make a puncture wound,
and tongue to lick up the bitsy blood.
A tiny prick never wakes up the sleeping cattle.
With draculin in my saliva, blood doesn't clot.
A clue to prevent strokes?

We are very social
and caring, neither harsh nor evil.
Vampire is such a false name.
We do not suck blood as our title implies.
But, I know
blood is blood,
name is name,
I live my life and die in shame.

Vulture

Unlike the human vulture, I do not
sell out my friends. I do not ambush, rob,
or set traps. With my keen eyesight, I can spot
a carcass miles away. I just do my job.

I circle the remains to signal my kith.
We are scavengers, never picky nor
fussy about the left overs, we share with
each other. That is what a friend is for.

We strip the rotten meat from the dead
that no one wants, our stomach acids kill
all bacteria and viruses to halt the spread
of diseases from rotting mort. It's our daily drill.

No need to thank me, just do not call me
vulture. Be fair, please accept my sincerest plea.

Philippine Eagle

They called me monkey-eating eagle. I eat
also civets, lizards, snakes on the ground,
and flying lemurs, birds, hornbills in the air.

I am Philippine national bird.
A strict punishment of twelve years
in prison for anyone who kills me.

Still, I am on the list of top ten most
endangered birds. Only hundreds left.
City expansion, habitats gone, I'm toast.

The largest eagle in the world with striking
appearance. A hunter's top prized trophy.
Dominant, yet vulnerable, I'm almost extinct.

I am running out of places to survive.
An apex predator, powerful and strong.
Yet, I barely hang on, don't know for how long.

Snipe

(It is a common belief that a snipe hunt is some sort of wild
goose chase. A fool's errand, a practical joke that experienced
people make fun of credulous newcomers by giving them an
impossible or imaginary task. The origin is inexperienced
campers are told about a bird called a snipe, and the method to
catch it. Such as running around the woods carrying a bag or
making strange noises such as banging rocks together.
Henry David Thoreau described the snipe's winnowing as a
"peculiar spirit-suggesting sound."*)

It is hard to say who I am.
I am best known as a fictional creature,
invented to send the newcomer
on a fool's errand.
Rest assured, I am a real bird.
The hunt confuses me too.

I have been here all along,
zoom into the sky
with a zigzag flight to sweep and clear
all the stories and tales
about a snipe hunt.

A sigh in the clouds, an outcry,
a mysterious winnowing call.
"A peculiar spirit-suggesting sound,"*
haunting and eerie.
In the twilight to leave
all the superstitions behind
in a drained and weary
journey to explore the folklore,
into the eve.

In search of the dim speck of me,
there is a real snipe
flying high,
a hunt worth to pry.

Mockingbird

(Harper Lee's book "To Kill a Mockingbird" was an all-time best seller, taught in school, one of the most widely read books.)

I am a great artist. Picasso said
"Good artists copy; great artists steal."
I mimic other birds' songs. When I was fed up
with those tunes, I composed my own with zeal.

And Harper Lee said "It is a sin to kill
a mockingbird. They don't eat up gardens, they just
sing their hearts out for us." A sign of goodwill.
Under the sun, I warble with my trill.

My name means "many-tongued mimic."
Mimicking is an ability, an art.
Chosen for Lee's book was not a gimmick.
On fences and wires, I am just doing my part.

I sing and make my presence known, I do
love my own music that keeps my voice true.

But I have promises to keep, and miles to go before I sleep, and miles to go before I sleep.

Robert Frost

Greater Roadrunner

I am born to run in the desert,
lean my frame nearly parallel to the ground,
rudder with long tails in the dusty shrubs,
I preen my mottled plumage
and make cooing sounds.

Making a living in the desert
is not for everyone.
The heat of the day,
the cold at night.
Scoop up anything you can bite:
insects, spiders, tarantulas, scorpions,
lizards, venomous serpents and mice.

And yes, beat up rattlesnakes.
And fly when coyote attacks.

Run, run,
in the gust.

Never settle,
in the dust.

Common Swift

My name is common swift,
yet, I'm so uncommon.
Unlike all the rest of the birds,
I'm on my wings to meet every need.
I eat, drink, preen and play.
And yes, mate and sleep too.
Almost all my life is in the air.
I stay airborne for extended periods.
Some say months, some say years.
It is an understatement to say
I am unique and rare.

I fly really high into the clouds, and then
slowly descend in circles, drop gently while
dozing off, wake up from air pressure when
I drop too low, and repeat with skill and style.

Scientists are paying attention to study
my sleeping mold and flair.
As insomnia is a muddy scare.

Christmas Island Frigatebird

I live on Christmas Island, a small
Australian territory in the Indian sea.
Isolated for millions of years, a wall
to the outside world, I'm as free as can be.

I love to fly and I can stay aloft for
more than a week. Stealing food in flight
from other seabirds is my daily chore.
A sky pirate, a terrorizing wright.

This is my island, this is my land.
Soaring like a condor of the ocean.
Everyday is a Christmas in my kingdom.

Inflating my bright red gular sac,
I attract and please my mate. Snatching fish
on the ocean's surface is a cinch.

I am on the endangered species list.
As long as there are fish in the sea,
I intend to enjoy every Christmas Eve.

Peregrine Falcon

What is the fastest animal in the world?
None can run like cheetah,
a car on the free-way.
Not a soul can swim faster than sailfish,
known to be as swift as a cheetah.

Humans invented airplane by studying how I fly.
A 240 mile dash in one hour.
Cheetah and sailfish get to the finish line in three.
Car against airplane, it is night and day.

The land and sky are my kingdoms.
I can live anywhere,
nesting on cliff edges is my choice.
High and no one can dispute.
I am the only voice.

We stay with our mates for life,
together we patrol our vast territory.
Free and glee.
In health, joy or strife.

Birds are a miracle because they prove to us there is a finer, simpler state of being which we may strive to attain.

Douglas Coupland

Kite

Striking shape and pattern at first sight,
I am the most beautiful bird of prey.
With extraordinary, graceful flight,
it is a joy to watch how I sail and play.

Swooping, gliding, rolling upside down,
sometimes, hanging motionless in the air,
as though I am performing for the town,
I zoom high into the clouds to their stare.

I am buoyant when I soar, slowly flap
and glide with wings angled back. They say I fly
like a kite, I say the kite stole my innate map.
Let wind be my wings, eyes aim high in the sky.

There is no reason to hash over who
copies whom. We need more kites in the blue.

Stork

Birth and death, comes and goes, soul lingers on.
We all know there is a soul, where is it?
In ancient Egypt I was linked with the soul.

I am faithful to my mate and to my nest.
Roman mythology portrayed me as a model
of parental love, a standard of filial value.

I am well respected. In Greece, it's a death
penalty if you kill me. German, Dutch
favor us to build nests, a large one on the roof.

Mascot, motif, I am also featured on
more than 120 stamps, issued by 60 entities.
National bird of Lithuania and Belarus.

Who else has so many blessings bestowed?
I can brag all day if I have a vocal organ.
Speechless, I am so grateful in my soul.

Flamingo

Pink is my color. Unique and rare.
A sea of flamingos is the colony of
thousands of my peers. All groom and wear
the same coat of unity and love.

It represents the identity and harmony,
same skin, same feathers, It must be the shrimp
we eat hence genesis, the pink, the destiny,
tied together since birth when we learned to limp.

Sounds cool. But, is this real? It must be a show.
The costume designer brings a whole army
of tailors to braid the elegant furbelows.

The choreography is simple. The vertical,
stiff ballet-legs, wade in the shallow wet land.
In the end, thousands of us take a bow.

Peacock

The work of my life is to leave the mark
on my tail. I erect the fan to display and flip
shimmering train, to show off and spark
the adoration to my gentlemanship.

A silver spoon in my mouth, it is a lore,
I became a darling of king and queen.
Duke, duchess treat me well, they all die for
my iridescent plumage, blue and green.

Sapphires and jewels, rubies and jades,
a glistening beauty contest every night.
Palace is my back yard, aides and maids,
surrounded by admirers, nobility is trite.

Again, babbling behind flabellum to plot,
once more, to count my each and every eyespot.

White Egret

(Derek Walcott is a poet. He won the 1992 Nobel Prize in literature.)

I am motionless when I stand in
the water to catch fish. I am fearless
when I perch on alligator's rugged skin.

In old times, I was hunted to near extinction.
My plumes were used to decorate ladies' hats.
White and gorgeous,
they were worth two-times weight in gold.
Kill us is all they do.

The plumes-fad faded, that saved my life.
No more guns or knives, I survive the ordeal.

Derek Walcott chose me as the title of
his book. Mary Oliver wrote about me.
The National Audubon society loves
my story. I became their symbol to plea.

Whooping Crane

I'm the tallest bird in North America.
Five feet tall.
A big target.
We were hunted until only 15 remained.

Our unison call is
a deep, rhythmic tune
in the early morning.
It galvanizes humans
just waking up with clear souls.

We became a symbol,
an inspiration.

A tireless effort to bring us back.
They built ultralight aircraft to guide us
in "operation migration."

We were pursued unto death,
and now rescued to live.
Do humans know
what they have done?
What they are doing?

An endangered species,
we still are.

We stand tall from all the scars.

The reason birds can fly and we can't is simply because they have perfect faith, for to have faith is to have wings.

J.M. Barrie

Hawk

Zooming in and out
like a laser beam.
A razor-sharp focus,
ignoring the rest of the world.
No compromise.
Solution is clear.

I circle and circle,
standstill to flap
my wings,
sustaining in the air
like a chopper, aim at my target,
pounce to snap and back.
A thunderbolt's strike.
Never ease off my stare.
Never waver or veer.

Hour, day, month,
year after year.

Osprey

Call me fish eagle or fish hawk.
I have the sharpest vision
of all living organisms on earth.

I see fish in my flight,
swoop down,
plunge into water,
well equipped;
waterproof oily feathers,
sealed nasal valves,
un-feathered long legs to keep me dry.

With backward facing barb-like scales
on my talons, I hook the fish.
My reversible toes align the fish head
to face forward
during my cruise home.

Back to my same old nest,
generation after generation,
breakfast, lunch or dinner,
I am the ultimate fisher of the sky.

Owl

I do not know where I belong.
Many natives see me as a symbol of
death, destruction and bad omens.
I am born to get lost in the forest.

I hide behind branches,
muffle my wings' beat,
like a stealth airplane, quiet and fleet.
No one cares to say hello or greet.

My confidence is gone, some link me
with wisdom, others to idiots, I am
confused as hell. All my life is to flee,
to elude, as though I conceal the flam.

Why do I exist? Where do I go from here?
Drear and fear, I stare all night, out of tear.

There is symbolic as well as actual beauty in the migration of the birds...the assurance that dawn comes after night, and spring after the winter...

Rachel Carson

Migratory Birds

When winds start to blow,
I follow the flock to migrate.
Flying overseas first time,
face the endless unknown.

Navigating by celestial cues
and magnetic forces. Big Dipper
shows one clear course.

A visitant becomes permanent.
A certificate to the vast resources,
bountiful food, the fulminant
first-time migration turns into the last.

A signal from heaven, it must be,
over the mountainous ridge and sea.

Swallow

We live in every cosmopolis,
from sea level to high alpines. I bite
insects as I glide, and in each metropolis,
I show my aerial acrobatic flight.

I am a good harbinger to sailors at sea.
I live on land, my showing-up is a clue
to sailors that they are just about to see
the shore, great news for every crew.

They call me the "bird of freedom," I cannot
endure captivity, and humans wish
they can be free like me. We have a lot
in common. Come and go, I fly by in a whish.

Abundant everywhere, sill, fence and balcony.
We love young and old, we are good company.

Oven Bird

("The Oven Bird" is a poem by Robert Frost. This poem was
written in sonnet form and describes an ovenbird singing.
"The question that he frames in all but words
Is what to make of a diminished thing."*
are the last two lines of the poem.)

I am such a common bird.
Female and male look alike,
both inconspicuous,
and our singing is below average,
nothing stands out.

My nest woven like an oven,
I leave it on the ground,
not smart? Wide open for predators?
They named me oven bird.
Bird in the oven?
Emboldens no poetic lore.
Everyone has doubt.

Not until Frost wrote a sonnet
"The Oven Bird,"
I became an overnight success.
My commonness turns into an inspiration
as they dwell,
"what to make of a diminished thing,"*
while my fortune had begun to sprout.

My series of strident,
repeated low-pitched motives' songs,
only Frost can explain what they mean,
as I ponder and conceal my clout.

Curlew

("The Tide Rises, The Tide Falls" is a poem by Henry
Wadsworth Longfellow.)

I am a wading bird. From shore to shore
I migrate, frequent dry uplands, feed on
insects and seeds. In the tides, I do my chore
to probe for worms, crayfish and crabs at dawn.

The curlew's call is the fabric of a dream.
Longfellow, my kind of fellow, likes my calls
near dusk, he mentioned in his traveler-theme
poem, my favorite, "The Tide Rises, The Tide Falls."

And the day goes by, the traveler on the go,
returns to the shore, and I move on to
another coast, another tide, high and low.
The darkness calls through the morning dew.

In the twilight glow, the migrators roam.
Through dreams and calls until he finds home.

About the Author

This was Livingston Rossmoor's second book of poetry. As of 2018, he has written and published 12 poetry books, 2 books of prose and poetry and 1 book of 13 short stories. He has also previously composed and produced 2 DVD's, and 1 CD.

Over his 40 year career in publishing, Livingston oversaw the production of 11 printed consumer magazines. He currently serves as the editorial director of the journal: *Nourish-Poetry* and is an associate member of the Academy of American Poets.

Rossmoor believes in service and is a long-time volunteer, working mostly with cancer patients. He currently resides in California with his dear wife of 45 years. He has 3 children and is the proud grandfather of 8 grandchildren.

So I Was Hired

March 2015

(I was quite ill for 18 months, but I came back with a renewed
spirit. After 36 years as a publisher of 11 magazines, I realize
sometimes, publisher is an ambiguous term, so I describe myself
as a chef.)

I was a chef for 36 years, cooked up
11 dishes in repertoire. And I got whupped
and burnt and fired many times,
they said I was too slow,
my time wasn't worth a dime.

But I need to support my
growing family, they said they don't
need me to buy the good ingredients,
that's too basic. I said I know how to use pot
and wok and cut every corner to fry
and cook cheaply, they said that is
just common sense.

To hold on to my job, they told me
"stupid, it is all in the presentation."
and I need to learn how to pitch and plea
these 11 dishes by segmentation,
direct mail, audio, video and radio,
free sampling, promote on the internet, sustentation
in stores and newsstands, and yes, television,
otherwise, I will be fired and on my knee.

I was a slow learner, got sick
because the kitchen was too hot.
I had to take a leave of absence
without my pay for 18 months. And I got
hired this morning again, they picked me,
and will try me for the last slot.